PI

# MOVIE MUSIC PAST & PRESENT

ISBN 0-634-01583-4

## HAL•LEONARD®
### CORPORATION
7777 W. BLUEMOUND RD. P.O. BOX 13819 MILWAUKEE, WI 53213

Visit Hal Leonard Online at
**www.halleonard.com**

# CONTENTS

# THEME FROM ANGELA'S ASHES

**Paramount Pictures and Universal Pictures International Present ANGELA'S ASHES**

Music by
JOHN WILLIAMS

**Gently flowing**

7

**Reflectively**

**With motion**

**Moderately**

# ANOTHER DUMB BLONDE

## from the Motion Picture SNOW DAY

Words and Music by ANTONINA ARMATO
and TIM JAMES

# THEME FROM ARMAGEDDON

## from the Touchstone Picture ARMAGEDDON

Music by TREVOR RABIN

**Deliberately**

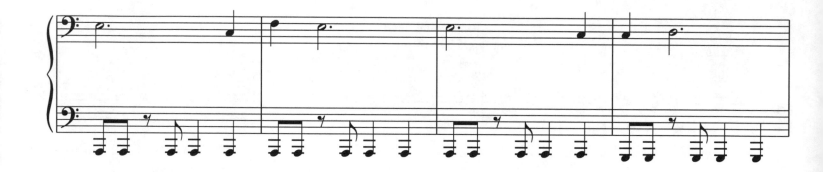

# BABY ELEPHANT WALK
## from the Paramount Picture HATARI!

Words by HAL DAVID
Music by HENRY MANCINI

Moderately slow and steady

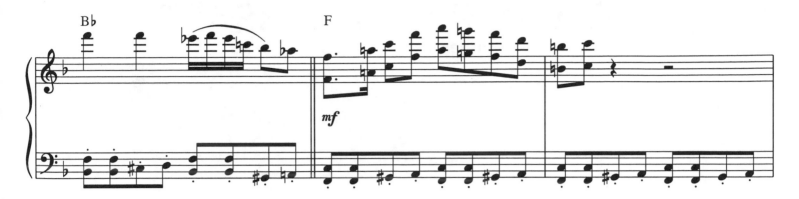

# BEAUTY AND THE BEAST
## from Walt Disney's BEAUTY AND THE BEAST

Lyrics by HOWARD ASHMAN
Music by ALAN MENKEN

# CAN'T HELP FALLING IN LOVE
from BLUE HAWAII

Words and Music by GEORGE DAVID WEISS,
HUGO PERETTI and LUIGI CREATORE

# THEME FROM "CASINO ROYALE"

from CASINO ROYALE

Words by HAL DAVID
Music by BURT BACHARACH

# CHARIOTS OF FIRE
## from CHARIOTS OF FIRE

Music by
VANGELIS

40

# THE CRYING GAME

## from THE CRYING GAME

Words and Music by
GEOFF STEPHENS

I know _ all there
*Instrumental solo*

# COLE'S SONG

## from MR. HOLLAND'S OPUS

Words by JULIAN LENNON and JUSTIN CLAYTON
Music by MICHAEL KAMEN

48

# DO YOU KNOW WHERE YOU'RE GOING TO?

Theme from MAHOGANY

Words by GERRY GOFFIN
Music by MIKE MASSER

Moderately, with expression

# THE ENGLISH PATIENT
## from THE ENGLISH PATIENT

Written by
GABRIEL YARED

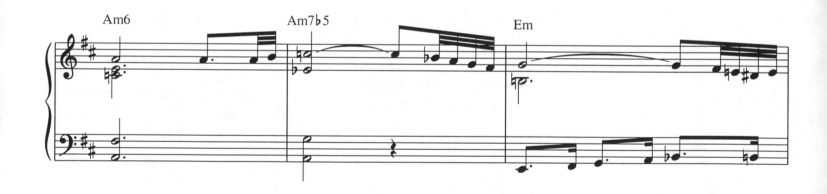

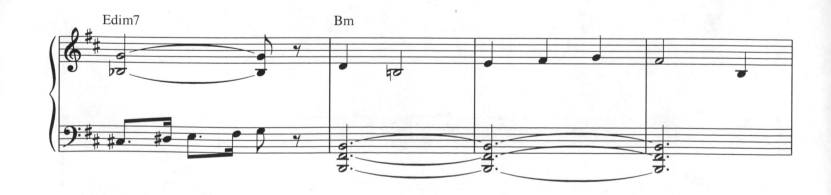

# EXHALE
## (Shoop Shoop)
### from the Original Soundtrack Album WAITING TO EXHALE

Words and Music by
BABYFACE

# THE FIRM – MAIN TITLE
## from the Paramount Motion Picture THE FIRM

By DAVE GRUSIN

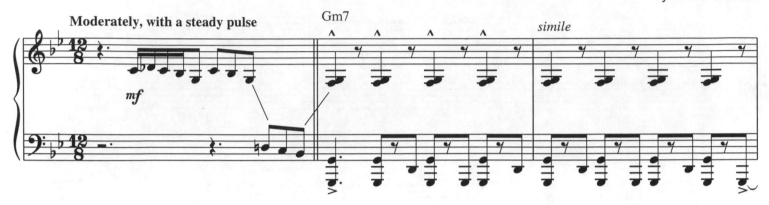

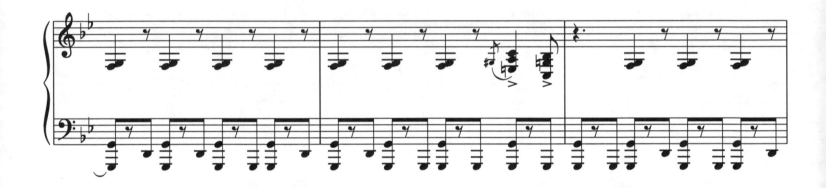

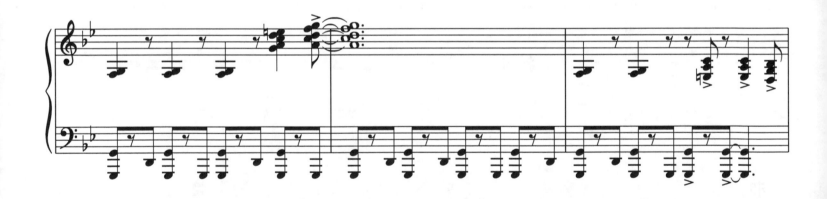

# FOOTLOOSE

## Theme from the Paramount Motion Picture FOOTLOOSE

Words by DEAN PITCHFORD and KENNY LOGGINS
Music by KENNY LOGGINS

70

I been work - in' ___ so hard. I'm punch - in'
You're play - in' ___ so cool, o - bey - ing

my ___ card. Eight hours, for what?
ev - 'ry rule. Dig way down in your heart

Oh, tell me what I got. I've got this
you're burn - in', yearn - in' for some, some - bod - y to

# A HARD DAY'S NIGHT

from A HARD DAY'S NIGHT

Words and Music by JOHN LENNON
and PAUL McCARTNEY

# I WILL REMEMBER YOU

## Theme from THE BROTHERS McMULLEN

Words and Music by SARAH McLACHLAN,
SEAMUS EGAN and DAVE MERENDA

# I LOVE YOU
## from the Paramount Motion Picture RUNAWAY BRIDE

Words and Music by TAMMY HYLER,
KEITH FOLLESE and ADRIENNE FOLLESE

# JAILHOUSE ROCK
## featured in the Motion Picture THE BLUES BROTHERS

Words and Music by JERRY LEIBER
and MIKE STOLLER

1. The war - den threw a par - ty in the
2.-5. *(See additional lyrics)*

coun - ty jail. ___ The pris - on band was there and they be -

gan to wail. The band was jump - in' and the joint be -

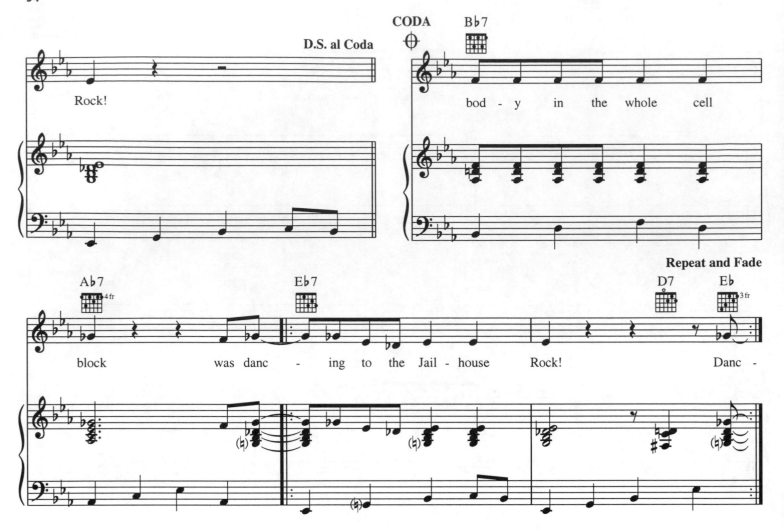

*Additional Lyrics*

2. Spider Murphy played the tenor saxophone
   Little Joe was blowin' on the slide trombone.
   The drummer boy from Illinois went crash, boon, bang;
   The whole rhythm section was the Purple Gang.
   *(Chorus)*

3. Number Forty-seven said to number Three:
   "You're the cutest jailbird I ever did see.
   I sure would be delighted with your company,
   Come on and do the Jailhouse Rock with me."
   *(Chorus)*

4. The sad sack was a-sittin' on a block of stone,
   Way over in the corner weeping all alone.
   The warden said: "Hey, Buddy, don't you be no square,
   If you can't find a partner, use a wooden chair!"
   *(Chorus)*

5. Shifty Henry said to Bugs: "For heaven's sake,
   No one's lookin', now's our chance to make a break."
   Bugsy turned to Shifty and he said: "Nix, nix;
   I wanna stick around a while and get my kicks."
   *(Chorus)*

# THEME FROM "LAWRENCE OF ARABIA"

from LAWRENCE OF ARABIA

By MAURICE JARRE

97

# THE JOHN DUNBAR THEME

### from DANCES WITH WOLVES

By JOHN BARRY

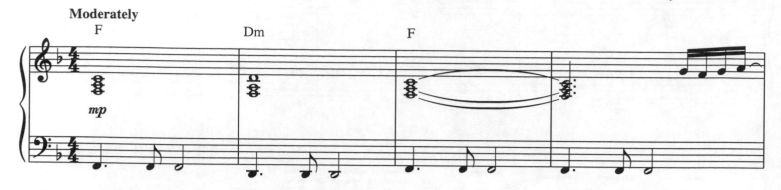

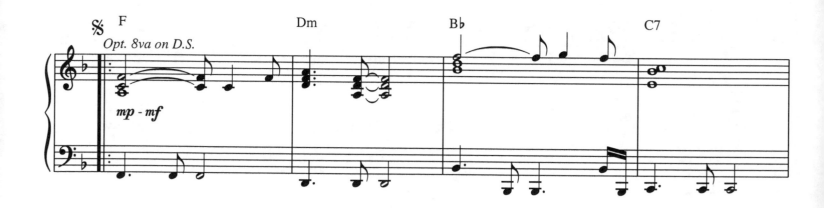

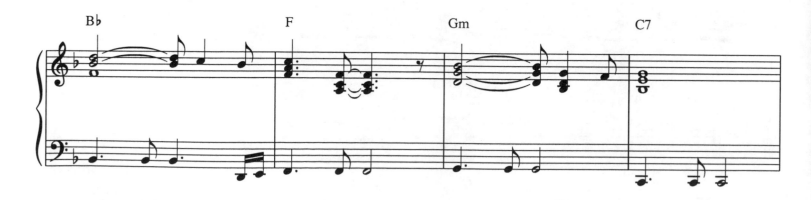

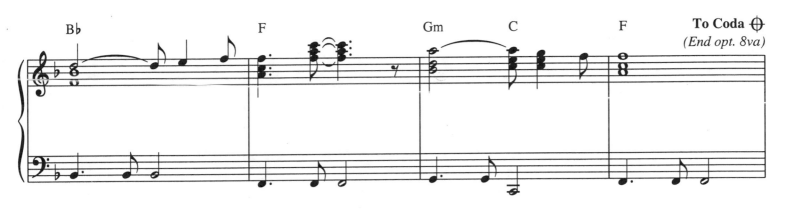

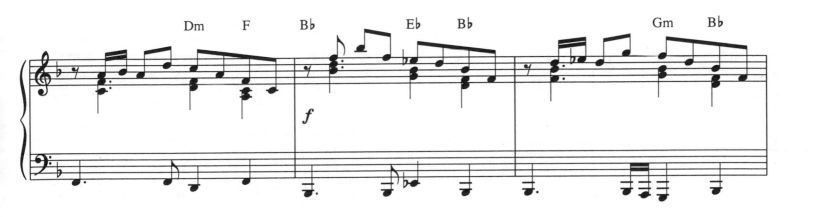

# LOOKIN' FOR LOVE

## from URBAN COWBOY

Words and Music by WANDA MALLETTE,
PATTI RYAN and BOB MORRISON

105

# MONEY, MONEY
## from the Musical CABARET

Words by FRED EBB
Music by JOHN KANDER

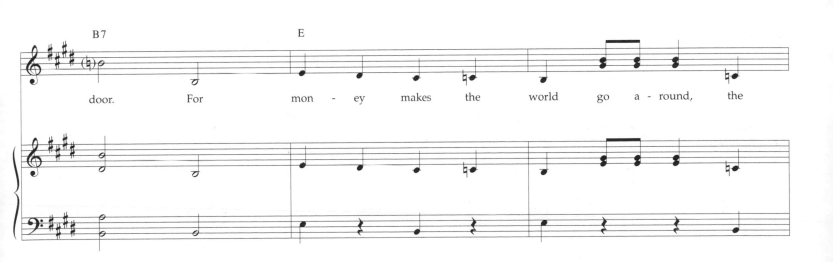

114

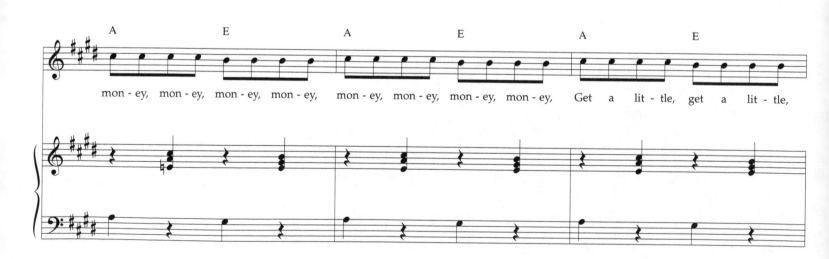

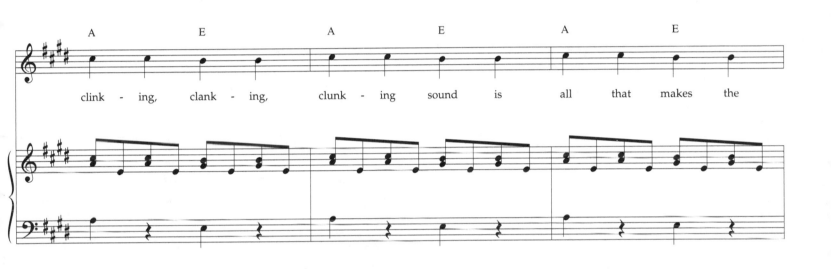

# LOVE ME OR LEAVE ME

## from LOVE ME OR LEAVE ME

Lyrics by GUS KAHN
Music by WALTER DONALDSON

# LULLABY FOR CAIN

from Paramount Pictures' and Miramax Films' THE TALENTED MR. RIPLEY

Lyrics by ANTHONY MINGHELLA
Music by GABRIEL YARED

# THE MAN FROM SNOWY RIVER
## (Main Title Theme)
### from THE MAN FROM SNOWY RIVER

By BRUCE ROWLAND

# MISSION: IMPOSSIBLE THEME

### from the Paramount Motion Picture MISSION: IMPOSSIBLE

By LALO SCHIFRIN

Moderate Dance beat, with drive

To Coda ⊕

129

# MOON RIVER
### from the Paramount Picture BREAKFAST AT TIFFANY'S

Words by JOHNNY MERCER
Music by HENRY MANCINI

# NIGHT FEVER
## from SATURDAY NIGHT FEVER

Words and Music by BARRY GIBB,
MAURICE GIBB and ROBIN GIBB

# MY HEART WILL GO ON
## (Love Theme from 'Titanic')
### from the Paramount and Twentieth Century Fox Motion Picture TITANIC

Music by JAMES HORNER
Lyric by WILL JENNINGS

140

# THE ODD COUPLE

## Theme from the Paramount Picture THE ODD COUPLE

Words by SAMMY CAHN
Music by NEAL HEFTI

# PSYCHO
## (Prelude)
### Theme from the Paramount Picture PSYCHO

Music by
BERNARD HERRMANN

Poco agitato

# RAIDERS MARCH

## from the Paramount Motion Picture RAIDERS OF THE LOST ARK

Music by JOHN WILLIAMS

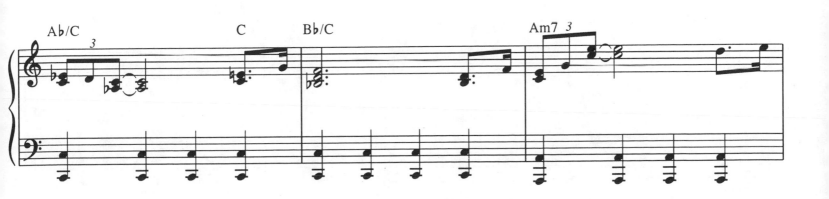

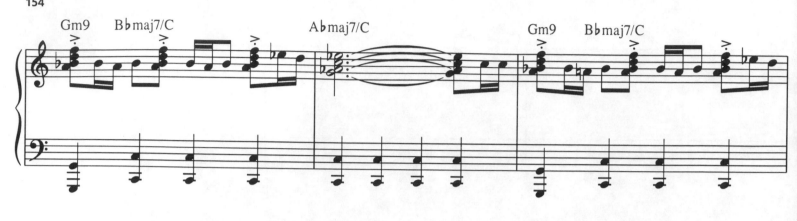

# RAINDROPS KEEP FALLIN' ON MY HEAD

## from BUTCH CASSIDY AND THE SUNDANCE KID

Lyric by HAL DAVID
Music by BURT BACHARACH

# THE RIVER KWAI MARCH

### from THE BRIDGE ON THE RIVER KWAI

By MALCOLM ARNOLD

# ROCK AROUND THE CLOCK
## featured in the Motion Picture BLACKBOARD JUNGLE

Words and Music by MAX C. FREEDMAN
and JIMMY DeKNIGHT

# ROMEO AND JULIET
## (Love Theme)
from the Paramount Picture ROMEO AND JULIET

By NINO ROTA

# SOMETHING GOOD
## from THE SOUND OF MUSIC

Lyrics and Music by
RICHARD RODGERS

**Coda**

# SOMETHING TO TALK ABOUT
## (Let's Give Them Something to Talk About)
from SOMETHING TO TALK ABOUT

Words and Music by
SHIRLEY EIKHARD

* Recorded a half step lower

# STAR TREK® THE MOTION PICTURE

Theme from the Paramount Picture STAR TREK: THE MOTION PICTURE

Music by JERRY GOLDSMITH

**Slowly**

**Power Rock shuffle**

178

# TEARS IN HEAVEN

### featured in the Motion Picture RUSH

Words and Music by ERIC CLAPTON
and WILL JENNINGS

Be-yond the door ___ there's peace, I'm sure, ___

# STEPPIN' OUT WITH MY BABY

from the Motion Picture Irving Berlin's EASTER PARADE

Words and Music by
IRVING BERLIN

# STORMY WEATHER
## (Keeps Rainin' All the Time)
### featured in the Motion Picture STORMY WEATHER

Lyric by TED KOEHLER
Music by HAROLD ARLEN

# THAT OLD BLACK MAGIC

from the Paramount Picture STAR SPANGLED RHYTHM

Words by JOHNNY MERCER
Music by HAROLD ARLEN

# THEN YOU LOOK AT ME

from Touchstone Pictures' and Columbia Pictures'
## BICENTENNIAL MAN (a Chris Columbus film)

Lyrics by WILL JENNINGS
Music by JAMES HORNER

*Original key: B major. This edition has been transposed down one half-step to be more playable.*

# THREE COINS IN THE FOUNTAIN

from THREE COINS IN THE FOUNTAIN

Words by SAMMY CAHN
Music by JULE STYNE

Three coins in the foun-tain, each one seek-ing hap-pi-ness, thrown by three hope-ful lov-ers, which one will the foun-tain bless? Three hearts in the foun-tain,

# TOP HAT, WHITE TIE AND TAILS

**from the RKO Radio Motion Picture TOP HAT**

Words and Music by
IRVING BERLIN

# THE WAY WE WERE

from the Motion Picture THE WAY WE WERE

Words by ALAN and MARILYN BERGMAN
Music by MARVIN HAMLISCH

# TRUE GRIT
## Theme from the Paramount Picture TRUE GRIT

Words by DON BLACK
Music by ELMER BERNSTEIN

# THE WORLD IS NOT ENOUGH

from the MGM Motion Picture THE WORLD IS NOT ENOUGH

Music by DAVID ARNOLD
Lyrics by DON BLACK

**Mysteriously, with a steady pulse**

220

# YOU'LL BE IN MY HEART
## (Pop Version)
### as performed by Phil Collins
### from Walt Disney Pictures' TARZAN™

Words and Music by
PHIL COLLINS

# YOU'RE WHERE I BELONG

## from the Columbia Pictures film STUART LITTLE™

Words and Music by
DIANE WARREN

# WHERE IS YOUR HEART
## (The Song from Moulin Rouge)
### from MOULIN ROUGE

Words by WILLIAM ENGVICK
Music by GEORGE AURIC

7/01